P9-BIK-305

Customer Service and the Telephone

DENNIS BECKER
PAULA BORKUM BECKER

Business Skills Express Series

McGraw-Hill

New York San Francisco Washington, D.C. Auckland Bogotá Caracas
Lisbon London Madrid Mexico City Milan Montreal New Delhi
San Juan Singapore Sydney Tokyo Toronto

McGraw-Hill

A Division of The McGraw·Hill Companies

© RICHARD D. IRWIN, INC., 1994

This publication is designed to provide accurate and
authoritative information in regard to the subject matter
covered. It is sold with the understanding that neither the
author or the publisher is engaged in rendering legal, accounting,
or other professional service. If legal advice or other expert
assistance is required, the services of a competent professional
person should be sought.

*From a Declaration of Principles jointly adopted by a Committee
of the American Bar Association and a Committee of Publishers.*

Library of Congress Cataloging-in-Publication Data
Becker, Dennis, 1942-
    Customer service and the telephone / Dennis Becker, Paula Borkum
Becker.
        p.   ⸱ cm. — (Business skills express series)
      ISBN 0-7863-0224-0
      1. Telephone in business.   2. Customer service.   3. Telephone
etiquette.   I. Becker, Paula Borkum.   II. Title.   III. Series.
HF5541.T4B43   1994
658.8'12—dc20   94–340

Printed in the United States of America
    5 6 7 8 9 0 ML 1

About the Authors

Dennis Becker and Paula Borkum Becker founded the Speech Improvement Company in 1964. This Boston-based firm specializes in communication training with a focus on business speaking. As speech coaches, the Beckers train individuals and corporations in presentation skills, customer service, management communication, sales training, and interpersonal skills development. The Beckers' clients have included Chase Manhattan Bank, TJ Maxx, Hit or Miss, Price Waterhouse, Gillette, Bull HN Information Systems, Polaroid, Sheraton, and Marriott Hotels. Paula Borkum Becker holds a PhD in business communication, and Dennis Becker completed his doctorate in media communications.

ABOUT THE BUSINESS SKILLS EXPRESS SERIES

This expanding series of authoritative, concise, and fast-paced books delivers high-quality training on key business topics at a remarkably affordable cost. The series will help managers, supervisors, and frontline personnel in organizations of all sizes and types hone their business skills while enhancing job performance and career satisfaction.

Business Skills Express books are ideal for employee seminars, independent self-study, on-the-job training, and classroom-based instruction. Express books are also convenient-to-use references at work.

PREFACE

In 1953 Jack Schwartz, one of America's first telephone trainers, wrote "How to Get More Business by Telephone." His book became a classic for training businesspeople on the use of the phone in a business setting. Forty years ago it took Jack Schwartz eight full pages to try to convince business professionals that they should respect the value of the telephone in their businesses. This thought can now be conveyed in eight words: **The telephone is your most important business machine.**

There can be absolutely no doubt that without the telephone, many or most businesses would fail. It is relatively impossible to be in business today without the effective use of the telephone. Telephones are fast, convenient, and relatively inexpensive. The telephone certainly can save time, effort, and stress. Companies that make and market telephones now make it possible to get a phone in every conceivable size, shape, and color. Phones can look like anything from your favorite fruit to your favorite movie star. You can have a phone anywhere—in your living room, at poolside, or even in your back pocket. Phones can ring, beep, buzz, light up, play music, or talk to you to let you know you have a call. You can dial them by rotary or keypad, or talk to them to tell them what to do. People use phones for everything—from fun to business, to arranging finance or funerals. In short, the telephone is life's most important business machine.

Now, phones are also fun and user-friendly. What more could we ask?

From a business standpoint we could ask, are we efficient and effective at using the phone? Do we use our familiarity with the phone to help business?

To answer these questions briefly, let's look at the results of an extensive research study done in 1992 by Technical Assistance Research Programs for The Society of Consumer Affairs Professionals in Business

(SOCAP/TARP). They reported on the use of 800 phone numbers, one of the most business oriented uses of the phone.

The report addresses an important and often asked question about providing special service to customers over the telephone: *"Does it make any difference?"*

The **SOCAP/TARP** research provides a clear answer to this question. When a customer merely has the opportunity to complain he or she will do business with you again up to 46 percent of the time. When your customers have the opportunity to complain, and the complaint is heard but not necessarily resolved, those customers will do business with you again up to 70 percent of the time. When your customer complains and the complaint is resolved quickly, that customer will do business with you again up to 95 percent of the time.

Customer	Will Return
Merely complains	46%
Complains but not resolved	70%
Complains and resolved quickly	95%

Telephone customer service works! In fact, it works two ways. You can either provide good service or bad service. Simply having the latest telephone technology will not guarantee good service. Good service is best delivered by people. It comes down to people serving people.

How do people learn to provide good service over the phone? In this book, we'll teach the ABC's of excellent customer service on the telephone.

We'll look at how **A** *attitudes* are developed, then learn how to improve **B**'s, your *behaviors*. Finally, we will make suggestions to help you follow up on your **C**'s, the *consequences* of your telephone service activity. Good luck!

Paula Borkum Becker
Dennis Becker

CONTENTS

Assessments

The following assessments will help you to determine the quality of your interactions with callers. The self-assessment will give you a picture of how you think you interact with callers. The observer-assessment will give you a picture of how your interactions are perceived by others. Comparing your results on both assessments will give you insight into how well you service your telephone callers and will suggest areas for improvement.

SELF-ASSESSMENT

For each of the 25 statements, place a check in the column that most accurately describes you.

	Never	Rarely	Some-times	Often	Always
1. I understand how important quality phone service is.	_____	_____	_____	_____	_____
2. I take an interest in servicing all callers.	_____	_____	_____	_____	_____
3. I separate my personal feelings from professional actions.	_____	_____	_____	_____	_____
4. I put a smile on my face and in my voice with each call.	_____	_____	_____	_____	_____
5. I know how to use all the features of my business phone.	_____	_____	_____	_____	_____
6. I control my biases.	_____	_____	_____	_____	_____
7. I do whatever it takes to make my caller happy and satisfied.	_____	_____	_____	_____	_____
8. I answer my calls within three rings.	_____	_____	_____	_____	_____
9. I control my speed of speaking.	_____	_____	_____	_____	_____

	Never	Rarely	Some-times	Often	Always
10. I pause between thoughts when speaking.	___	___	___	___	___
11. I give accurate and complete messages.	___	___	___	___	___
12. I take accurate and complete messages.	___	___	___	___	___
13. I maintain a person-able voice.	___	___	___	___	___
14. I listen actively and attentively.	___	___	___	___	___
15. I do not interrupt callers.	___	___	___	___	___
16. I use clear articulation.	___	___	___	___	___
17. I control my speaking volume for the situation.	___	___	___	___	___
18. I vary my inflection and tone when expressing myself.	___	___	___	___	___
19. I carefully choose appropriate language.	___	___	___	___	___
20. I am courteous at all times.	___	___	___	___	___
21. I empathize with my callers.	___	___	___	___	___
22. I am enthusiastic in my responses to callers.	___	___	___	___	___
23. I practice my phone servicing out loud.	___	___	___	___	___
24. I practice my phone servicing on tape.	___	___	___	___	___
25. I strive to give amazing phone service.	___	___	___	___	___

Scoring

Give yourself a zero for each Never, one point for each Rarely, two points for each Sometimes, three points for each Often, and four points for each Always. Add the totals for all five columns and determine your total score. How did you do?

100–90   A+: You are doing an amazing job of servicing your callers. Make sure your observer-assessment score matches your score here. There may still be room for improvement.

89–75   B: You are doing an above-average job of servicing your customers. You will find the many suggestions in this book will help you become an A+ performer.

74–50   C: You are doing an average job of servicing your customers. This book will help you improve your servicing skills, enhancing your business at the same time.

49–30   D: Your phone-servicing skills are deficient. This book will help you understand the importance of good phone-servicing skills and will give you skills critical for business success.

29–0   F: Your phone-servicing skills are almost nonexistent and in great need of repair. This book will help you build a foundation for becoming a good phone servicer.

OBSERVER-ASSESSMENT

Identify a co-worker who is familiar with your phone-servicing style. Have him or her observe your servicing style over the period of a week and then complete the items below by placing a check in the column that most accurately describes you for each of the 25 statements.

	Never	Rarely	Some-times	Often	Always
1. Understands how important quality phone service is.					
2. Takes an interest in servicing all callers.					
3. Can separate personal feelings from professional actions.					
4. Puts a smile on her or his face and in the voice with each call.					
5. Knows how to use all the features of the business phone.					
6. Controls personal biases.					
7. Does whatever it takes to make the caller happy and satisfied.					
8. Responds to calls within three rings.					
9. Controls his or her speed of speaking.					
10. Pauses between thoughts when speaking.					
11. Gives accurate and complete messages.					
12. Takes accurate and complete messages.					
13. Maintains a personable voice.					
14. Listens actively and attentively.					
15. Does not interrupt callers.					
16. Uses clear articulation.					
17. Controls her or his speaking volume appropriately, depending on the situation.					
18. Varies inflection and tone when expressing himself or herself.					

	Never	Rarely	Some-times	Often	Always
19. Carefully chooses appropriate language.	_____	_____	_____	_____	_____
20. Is courteous at all times.	_____	_____	_____	_____	_____
21. Is empathetic with callers.	_____	_____	_____	_____	_____
22. Is energetic in her or his responses.	_____	_____	_____	_____	_____
23. Practices phone servicing out loud.	_____	_____	_____	_____	_____
24. Practices phone servicing on tape.	_____	_____	_____	_____	_____
25. Strives to give amazing phone service.	_____	_____	_____	_____	_____

Scoring

To score the observer-assessment, use the same scoring instructions as in the self-assessment. Note carefully any differences in outcome between the two measurements, and plan to improve upon any weaknesses that either you or your observer identify.

1 | Who's Who on the Phone?

This chapter will help you to:

- Distinguish between customers and clients.
- Differentiate between personal and professional attitudes and behaviors.
- Understand the five levels of human needs.
- Distinguish between external and internal callers.

May I help you?

I'd like to order five single-slide bolt locks.

What size and color?

Six inches in polished gold.

OK. What's your account number?

DPA 773.

OK. I see your name and address on my record from your last purchase. Would you like these locks sent to the same address?

Yes. What's the shipping cost?

Total with shipping is $97.50.

How long will it take?

They should arrive in three to four days.

Thank you. That's fine.

Thank you. Bye.

Bye. ∎

Focusing on client relationships, with an emphasis on getting to know the client, makes good business sense.

WHO IS BEING SERVED?

The words *customer* and *client* frequently are used interchangeably, but they actually refer to different things. Not only will you make a mistake by confusing customers with clients, but also you may alienate the very person you are trying to serve. Service expectations and delivery differ depending on which you are serving.

Customers are:

- People who expect and should receive a direct, efficient, immediate, and appropriate response.

1

- People you may not know, may never have seen, nor will ever see again.
- People with whom you have a short, quick, and impersonal interaction.

Clients are:

- People who expect and should receive a direct, efficient, immediate, and appropriate response.
- People who can be found in the offices of service professionals such as accountants and attorneys.
- People who you must get to know.
- People with whom you must have a *relationship*.

The difference between customer service and client service relates to the type of relationship found in each. Client relationships require considerable time and effort to develop. Your client expects a certain level of service delivered in a certain way, especially when the cost of your service is high. Customers, on the other hand, expect equally good service but delivered differently. One of your most important tasks is to determine whether you are serving a customer or a client. Whichever you are serving, your service at a minimum must be direct, efficient, immediate, and appropriate, within a customer or client's expectations. The degree to which you exceed those expectations will dictate the satisfaction that you achieve.

Hints

Create two columns on a blank piece of paper. Label one *Customer* and the other *Client*. In the appropriate column, list the names of companies or people who serve you as either a customer or client. Remember, the determining factor is the relationship you have with them.

A final thought on who is being served relates to the concept of internal and external customers or clients. *External* customers or clients are people from outside your organization who require your service. *Internal* customers or clients are people within your organization who require your service.

Most service professionals are aware they must attend to the needs of the external customer or client. Do not, however, overlook the needs of your internal customer or client. The techniques found in this book will serve both.

WHO IS SERVING?

When you answer the phone and provide service to a caller, who is really doing the serving? Is it the *personal* you or the *professional* you? Actually, it is both. When you are at work serving people over the phone, you are utilizing your best professional skills. This is as it should be. But all too often you are not aware of personal influences or you are not in control of them.

When you are confronted by an upset caller who is accusatory, verbally abusive, or downright nasty, how do you respond? Do you continue to see yourself as a professional service provider or do you feel like you have just been personally attacked? Who responds—the personal you who feels attacked or the professional you who recognizes the situation? It can be very difficult to hear abusive language from threatening and intimidating callers. Professional service providers understandably often have personal reactions to abusive treatment. Nonetheless, you must learn to control your personal reactions and handle these situations with professional skill.

The professional ability to control personal reactions while meeting or exceeding your caller's expectations is the ability to be *personable*. This is the bridge between being personal and professional.

Check yourself. How do you react and respond? Can you maintain your professional composure when your instincts cry out for vengeance? You can if you learn the attitudes and behaviors inherent in a personable style of service. This book is all about being personable.

■ **Try This**

Read the following caller's comment. If you received this comment, how would you react—personally or professionally? How should you react? Check the examples given below, then write at least two of your own. Writing the personal response may feel good, but it is your professional response that is correct and more effective.

> *Every time I call you people, I get the same thing. It's the runaround, and you're no different. I should just report your stupidity to your boss and take my business elsewhere.*

> Personal Response: *You don't have to talk to me like that. I don't even know who you are, so back off.*

> Professional Response: *I'm sorry you are unhappy with our service. I'll do my best to change that. How may I help you?*

Your Response 1 _____

_____

Your Response 2 _____

_____

WHAT IS BEING SERVED?

Callers express a variety of wants and needs for service. Your job as a service provider is to respond to those needs and wants appropriately.

The Business Level

Wants are those things that would be nice to have, would be helpful to have, would make life easier, or would add benefit to the service. *Needs* are those things that the call for service requires. Examples of some wants and needs include these:

Wants	Needs
Delivery by Monday.	Delivery by Thursday.
Billing every week.	Billing every month.
Repairs completed this week.	Repairs completed next week.

These wants and needs are not too difficult to identify. You can then design and deliver appropriate service. Remember, always *try* to meet the wants; always *do* meet the needs.

The Human Level

Your callers are not only customers or clients; they are people, and people have some basic human needs. You may not always be able to identify your callers' needs, but you should always keep them in mind. Listen for opportunities to meet these needs.

All people share five levels of basic human needs (first formally identified by psychologist Abraham Maslow).

Level 1: Life. To be alive and healthy enough to function.

Level 2: Safety and security. To feel safe and secure where you live and work (this level of need includes the need for job security).

Level 3: Belonging and affection. To be part of a group of other human beings at work, on teams, and in families and to feel liked by those around you.

Level 4: Respect and self-respect. To have the professional respect of those around you for the talents and skills you possess, to feel personal respect, and to accept yourself as a worthy contributor.

Level 5: Self-actualization. To reach the point where all your other needs have been met so you no longer feel needy and you know you have reached your full potential.

■ **Try This**

Choose a customer or client you know well. If this is not possible, generalize to all your customers or clients. Place a check in the appropriate column to indicate whether or not your company's product or service satisfies the specific customer and client needs that correspond to the five basic human needs.

	Yes	No
1. Does your product or service promote the physical or psychological health or well-being of your customers or clients?		
2. Does your product or service promote a safer work or living environment or a more secure social or business position for your customers and clients?		
3. Does your product or service promote the feeling among your customers and clients that they are liked or that they are part of an organization that is accepting and appreciative?		
4. Does your product or service promote the feeling that your customers or clients are recognized for technical or professional capabilities?		
5. Does your product or service promote the belief that all your customers' and clients' needs are being met and that they are completely satisfied?		

In answering the question "What is being served?" recognize that you may be serving several needs at the same time. Use the professional skills outlined in this book to help you identify, appropriately meet, and exceed the expectations and needs of those you serve.

Chapter 1 Checkpoints

✓ Does your organization serve customers, clients, or both?

✓ Can you identify your internal and external clients? Who are they?

✓ Can you control personal attitudes and behaviors?

✓ What human needs does your service respond to?

2 | Attitudes and Approaches

This chapter will help you to:

- Understand the five ways that attitudes are developed.
- Identify five specific service approaches.
- Assess your own service attitude.

Hey, Dylan, would you take the call on line 3? Everybody else is busy. It's a service information call.

Why me? I'm busy with something else. Tell them to hold.

Come on Dylan, I don't want to pick it up. They'll just ask me things.

For crying out loud! Don't these people know that a customer service department has other things to do besides answer the phone all day? We'd get a lot more done around here if these phones would stop ringing. OK, I'm coming. Hello, this is Dylan. May I help you? ■

■ Questions to Consider

1. Have you heard this attitude expressed before?

   _____

   _____

   _____

2

2. Have *you* actually expressed this attitude before?

_____

_____

_____

This chapter discusses the importance of attitude in delivering effective service over the phone.

ATTITUDES

Attitudes are developed in five major ways. Understanding all five contributing factors may help you understand your own attitude toward the delivery of service, although you will feel more comfortable with some ways than with others.

1. Observation.   As a very young child you observed parents, family, friends working, speaking, and interacting with others. As you observed their behavior, you were developing attitudes that would later shape your behavior in similar situations.

> *Example: You observed your parents' treatment of the service person who came to fix your refrigerator. You observed their language, tone of voice, and behavior before, during, and after his or her visit.*

2. Experience.   Early in life you experienced service that shaped your attitude. Rather than just observing, you actually participated in the service experience.

> *Example: You were sent to the store to buy milk and bread. The service treatment you received had an impact on your delivery of service as an adult.*

3. Teaching.   As a child you were taught by adults what attitudes were appropriate in given situations. As an adult you still may be learning attitudes from those around you.

Example: Have you heard fellow employees say "Don't work so hard, you make the rest of us look bad" or "You can go easy on this part; no one checks up on you"?

4. Peers.   As a child you were strongly influenced by the attitudes and behaviors of other children. Peer pressure is a well documented and accepted contributing factor to the development of attitudes. But peer pressure is not limited to childhood experiences; adults also are influenced by the attitudes and behaviors of their peers.

Example: Many adults prefer to eat the same foods, wear the same clothes, drive the same cars, and frequent the same places as others because "it's the thing to do."

5. Personality.   Your inborn personality, independent of any life experiences, strongly affects the attitudes you hold. At some point in your life you must accept responsibility for these attitudes. You cannot simply attribute them to childhood happenings.

Example: Are you still saying things like "But that's the way I was brought up" or "We've always done it that way"?

APPROACHES

 Try This

To help you assess your service attitudes, read the following five situations that require service. Each situation is followed by five optional service approaches labeled A, B, C, D, and E. After reading each situation, rank the approaches from 1 (most effective) to 5 (least effective). Place your number rankings on the blank lines.

Situation 1.   A caller objects vehemently to having his service changed due to nonpayment. He has exceeded your organization's grace period for payment of his bill.

2

_____ A. I would tell him that the grace period has expired and the organization's policy is "no money, no service."

_____ B. Because there is nothing I can do at this point, I would remain noncommitted.

_____ C. I think it best to avoid getting the caller more upset than he already is. I would try to sympathize with him and tell him I understand his position.

_____ D. I would try to calm him down and explain the organization's policy. Then I would indicate a willingness to help him get his service restored.

_____ E. I would attempt to determine why the bill has not been paid. If his explanation seems plausible, I would determine how best to secure payment and restore service.

Situation 2. A caller complains that a member of your organization promised to send her important materials within two or three days. It is now nearly two weeks later. The caller has been trying to reach the person who made the promise, but her calls are not returned and she needs the materials.

_____ A. I would agree that the service was inadequate and promise to send the materials out immediately.

_____ B. I would apologize for the inconvenience and explain that the materials would be sent as soon as possible.

_____ C. I would sympathize with the caller, get her phone number, and explain that I would call her back as soon as I could determine when the materials could be sent out.

_____ D. I would ask the caller to check her records again to be certain of the agreement to send the materials. Then I would urge her to recheck the mail and the post office. Perhaps the materials have simply been misdirected.

_____ E. I would tell the caller that I'll look into the problem, and pursue an explanation for the inconvenience, but make no commitment regarding the materials.

Situation 3. A caller is misrouted to you. She states that for the second time in four months she has been sent an incorrect computerized bill. She is very upset and makes abusive remarks concerning your firm.

_____ A. I would hear her out and then tell her that because I cannot resolve the problem, I will transfer her to the accounting department.

_____ B. Because her abusiveness is not helping to solve the problem, I would interrupt her and explain that with so many billings to be processed the computer is bound to make some errors.

_____ C. I would express regret over the mistake and promise to put her in touch with someone who can resolve her problem.

_____ D. I would apologize for the inconvenience and offer to transfer her to the proper party. Then I would follow up with organizational personnel and the caller to make certain the problem gets straightened out.

_____ E. I would be sympathetic and promise the caller that I would personally look into the matter, assuring her that such a mistake would not be made again.

Situation 4: A new caller is upset because your organization charges for services he thinks should be free or included as part of other fees.

_____ A. I would patiently explain that the charges are company policy and that the quality of service will far outweigh them.

_____ B. I would tell him that this policy applies to all clients and that all similar companies have the same charges.

_____ C. I would apologize and explain that I know how he feels. Further, I would assure him that we will provide the services promptly and that he will be pleased.

_____ D. I would explain the reason for the policy—in the past clients have exploited our complimentary services. Even though I am sure he would not do that, the company has established this policy to protect itself as much as possible.

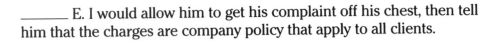

_____ E. I would allow him to get his complaint off his chest, then tell him that the charges are company policy that apply to all clients.

Situation 5.   You pass by the telephone receptionist and overhear her say, "I can't help it that you can't get an answer on that line. You don't have to be abusive with me. Call back later please."

_____ A. I would tell the receptionist that she has no right to talk to a caller that way. After all, the caller comes first—he's our bread and butter.

_____ B. I would ask her to explain what caused her to become so upset. I would suggest that if it happens again, she should offer to call the person back when the line is open. Then I would tactfully reinforce her importance as part of the company's overall image.

_____ C. I wouldn't say anything. Often callers can be irrational and rude. In addition, because of the quality of training that the organization provides, the receptionist probably would ignore my suggestion anyway.

_____ D. I would tell her that although callers can often be a pain in the neck, she should not do anything to tarnish the company's reputation. Getting upset and returning abusive behavior will give us a bad name.

_____ E. I would explain that neither the caller nor the organization wins when a situation like this gets out of hand and that she would not want to give the company a bad name.

The following five service approaches correspond to the five options provided for each of the preceding service situations. They are listed from the *most* effective to the *least* effective.

We Can Work It Out

This attitude and approach stresses maximum concern for both the caller and the organization. It is a problem-solving approach that utilizes objective criteria for satisfying the caller's needs while being aware of the organization's capabilities. This attitude and approach is patient and inductive, reserving judgment until all facts are known.

Make Nice

This attitude and approach expresses a moderate concern for both the caller and the organization. On balance, however, the organization comes first. Every effort is made to be nice to the caller, making him or her feel good about the communication.

You're #1

This attitude and approach shows maximum concern for the caller and minimum concern for the organization. Peace and happy coexistence with the caller are of the utmost importance, even if the organization assumes a cost or seems like the guilty party.

We're #1

This attitude and approach shows minimum concern for the caller and maximum concern for the organization. It tends to discount caller complaints or concerns while restating the organization's policy.

Take It or Leave It

This approach shows no concern for the caller and only little concern for the organization. Conflict, frustration, and irritation are inevitable.

ASSESSING YOUR SERVICE ATTITUDE

You should recognize that each caller will have an individual mixture of wants, needs, history, and extenuating circumstances. A single, simple approach will not work in every case. Therefore, in choosing the most effective service approach in each of the preceding five situations, you may have allowed for special conditions. The most effective service approaches for each situation presented are as follows:

SITUATION 1	E—We can work it out D—Make nice C—You're #1 B—Take it or leave it A—We're #1
SITUATION 2	C—We can work it out B—Make nice A—You're #1 D—We're #1 E—Take it or leave it
SITUATION 3	D—We can work it out C—Make nice E—You're #1 B—We're #1 A—Take it or leave it
SITUATION 4	D—We can work it out A—Make nice C—You're #1 B—We're #1 E—Take it or leave it
SITUATION 5	B—We can work it out E—Make nice A—You're #1 D—We're #1 C—Take it or leave it

As you can see, the "we can work it out" approach is always the best starting point for providing satisfying customer service. Keep this in mind as you work with clients, customers, and co-workers every day. The win-win solution benefits everyone.

Chapter 2 Checkpoints

✓ What is your attitude toward providing customer service to callers?

✓ How did that attitude develop?

✓ How close are you to the "we can work it out" approach?

3 | The Sound of Service

This chapter will help you to:

- Identify the most important elements of speaking clearly on the phone.
- Learn seven speech and voice techniques to use during calls.

PERRYNCATHRINZBUSTOURSNTRAVELNIHELBYOU.

Do you go to Atlantic City?

YEH. CANYOUHOLDONI'LLGESOMEONEWHONOZBOUDAT.

Well, I only need to know the times and costs.

OKIFYALEMMEGESOMEBIDDYWHOZSPONSBLTHELLTELYAHOLON. ■

■ Question to Consider

What did he say?

_____

_____

_____

You probably have had an experience like the one above—you hear something on the other end of the phone line that sounds like human speech, but not like any language you have ever heard. Such a call can be both puzzling and angering, and it gives a very poor impression of the person answering the call and of the company. The sound of service is frequently as important as the service itself. At times, it is even more important. This chapter provides specific techniques to avoid sounding like the person speaking in the opening dialogue. By the way, this is what the caller should have heard:

Perry and Catherine's Bus Tours and Travel. Can I help you?

Do you go to Atlantic City?

Yes, Can you hold on? I will get someone who knows about that.

Well, I only need to know the times and costs.

OK. Well, if you let me get somebody who is responsible, they will tell you. Hold on. ∎

On the phone, you project your company's image. In fact, on the phone, you *are* your company. People who call for information or assistance will judge your company by the treatment they receive. That "treatment" is communicated by the way you talk to them, by the way you sound on the phone. Speaking clearly is always important. Speaking clearly on the phone is absolutely imperative. It not only helps ensure accuracy and efficiency, it also helps promote a positive, professional image for your company.

Without the benefit of the visual cues you get and give through facial expression and body language, it is critical that your voice and speech be as controlled as possible. For better or worse, callers will judge the quality of the phone service in part by the way you sound. Seven voice and speech techniques will help you sound professional and personable on the phone.

SUPPORTING TECHNIQUE 1: Voice

Voice and speech are not the same even though many people use the terms interchangeably. *Voice,* simply explained, is the sound you are able to produce. *Speech* is what you do with your voice. Everyone has a unique voice determined by many elements, including the size of your vocal mechanism, your exercise routine, how you use your voice, and even your diet. Although you may not have any control over some of these factors, you can significantly affect many others.

Five valuable exercises can help you strengthen and control your voice.

▮ T r y   T h i s

Hyoid Exercise

Your hyoid muscles are connected to the lower part of your jawbone and the hyoid bone, which is at the top of your larynx or voice box. These muscles help control the movement of your vocal folds. You use them constantly for everything from swallowing to chewing to speaking. As a result, these muscles can become tense, in turn making the sound of your voice tight, higher pitched, and generally unrelaxed. To help your hyoid muscles remain strong and relaxed, you must stretch them. Do the following exercise for approximately one minute five times a day.

1. Lower your chin toward your chest.
2. Stop talking, chewing, and swallowing.
3. Using fingertips, gently push the hyoid muscles upward. Do not rub or massage them from side to side.
4. Stretch the entire area extending from directly under your chin to the end of the jawbone near your ear.

Humming Exercise

This exercise will help strengthen control of your vocal mechanism. Be sure to follow the steps in the order listed below. You will need approximately five minutes of uninterrupted time to complete the exercise. Repeat the entire process three times throughout the day.

1. Inhale naturally. Take in your normal amount of air.
2. As you exhale, say the sound *hum* at your normal speaking volume.

3. Maintain a set volume and try to sustain the hum throughout the duration of the exhalation.

4. Listen for "bumble beeing"—a fluttering sound much like that made by a bumble bee.

5. Try to eliminate as much "bumble beeing" as possible throughout the exhalation.

Sighing Exercise

This exercise will help you both relax and strengthen the vocal mechanism itself. You must follow the prescribed order to achieve maximum benefit. Allow yourself approximately five minutes of uninterrupted time. Repeat the exercise three times throughout the day.

1. Inhale naturally. Take in your normal amount of air.

2. As you exhale, very softly produce a sigh, using the sound "ah-h-h."

3. Maintain the sound throughout the exhalation.

4. The sigh should descend—that is, it should become softer and softer as you exhale.

5. Try to maintain the gentle sound of the sigh throughout the entire exercise.

Diaphragmatic Breathing Exercise

This exercise is crucial for increasing the control of your vocal strength and quality. Diaphragmatic breathing is the most appropriate form of breathing for speaking on the phone. You will need approximately five minutes to do the exercise. Repeat the exercise three separate times throughout the day.

1. Sit or stand comfortably in front of a mirror, if possible, so you can observe yourself.

2. Use your fingertips to push lightly on your diaphragm, located beneath your rib cage and above your belt line. Feel the movement as you breathe.

3. Inhale slowly through your nose or mouth. Feel the diaphragm move out. Your shoulders and upper chest should not move.

4. Hold this inhalation for three seconds.

5. As you exhale, count to 20 by saying "one by one, two by two, three by three," until you reach 20.

6. Stop whenever the exhalation becomes a strain.

7. If you do not reach 20 on one breath, repeat this exercise 10 times. Do this exercise three times daily until you reach 20 comfortably.

8. Lay on your back, placing a book on your abdominal muscles over your diaphragm. As you inhale, the book will rise up. As you exhale, the book will go down. Increase the weight by adding more books. Over time, you'll strengthen your diaphragm muscle.

Exercise and Diet

Several pointers will help you protect your voice and strengthen the overall physical conditions that affect the voice you use on the phone.

1. Avoid using dairy products such as milk, cheese, butter, and ice cream when you are using the phone. They coat the vocal folds and cause unnecessary congestion, poor vocal quality, and frequent throat clearing.

2. Avoid caffeine products such as coffee, tea, chocolate, and soft drinks while using the phone. They cause unnecessary tenseness in your vocal mechanism.

3. Avoid drinking or eating anything that is either very hot or very cold. These items negatively affect the flexibility of your articulators and your clarity of speech over the phone.

4. Avoid shouting, screaming, or other vocal strains. These activities damage your vocal folds and cause discomfort and loss of strength and clarity over the phone.

5. Sit or stand in a comfortable and erect position when speaking on the phone to ensure a clear flow of air through the vocal mechanism and allow better control and quality of sound.

3

6. Exercise by aerobic walking for 15 to 20 minutes at least three times a week. Begin by breathing diaphragmatically for the first five minutes of the walk. Aerobic walking helps strengthen your breath control for increased volume and quality over the phone.

SUPPORTING TECHNIQUE 2: Articulation

Articulation is the production of individual sounds. When you produce any one of the more than 50 sounds in the English language, you are articulating. Good articulation is the key to speaking clearly on the telephone. You may not be able to control the telephone equipment, the quality of the transmission, the strength of the signal, or the caller's environment. But you can control the clarity, quality, strength, and accuracy of your articulation. These exercises will improve your ability to speak clearly while providing service over the phone.

◼ Try This

1. Open your mouth wide and close it. This is a stretching exercise.
2. Round your lips, protrude them as far as you can, and practice the sound *oo* (5 times).
3. Spread your lips back in a *big* smile. Feel the muscles pulling around your chin and neck. Practice the sound *e* (5 times). Then practice the sounds *e-o, e-o* (10 times).
4. Thrust your upper lip forward. Thrust your lower lip forward (5 times).
5. Raise the right side of your mouth. Raise the left side of your mouth. Be sure your whole face is involved in the movement. The muscles of your face must move freely for expression (5 times).
6. Protrude your tongue without touching either your top lip or your bottom lip. This will be helpful to produce sounds such as *th* (10 times).

7. Point the tip of your tongue up and touch your top lip, then the right corner of your mouth, then the left. Complete the exercise by pointing your tongue down toward your chin (10 times).

8. Rotate your tongue around the inside of your mouth over your upper teeth, then your bottom teeth (10 times).

9. Raise the tip of your tongue and touch the gum ridge behind your upper front teeth. Slowly bring your tongue toward your soft palate (10 times).

10. Let the tip of your tongue touch the roof of your mouth. Flap it up and down, producing a strong *la, la, la, la* (10 times).

11. Practice opening your mouth as wide as you can to the point that you feel a tingling sensation (10 times).

12. Say the vowel sounds A-E-I-O-U in an exaggerated manner, stretching and overarticulating each sound. When done correctly, you will feel a tingling sensation in your cheeks, jaw, and neck (10 times).

SUPPORTING TECHNIQUE 3: Assimilation

Assimilation is the running together of words or sounds. It is common and accepted in informal, casual, and nondirected everyday conversation. A business call, on the other hand, is a formal and directed contact with your customer or client. The call has a purpose. Often the caller does not know how you speak. In this situation assimilation can cause problems. You, your company, and your phone service may be perceived as sloppy, careless, and unprofessional. What do you think when you place a call that is answered "brusncathsfosoiopzho" instead of "Bruce and Cathy's photo studio, please hold." To control assimilation, practice saying these words and phrases at your normal speaking speed. If you hear any assimilation, repeat the words, articulating each sound more carefully. Practice this technique on an answering machine or voice mail to hear what your caller will hear. Remember, articulation exercises help control common assimilations.

Want to—not wanna.

Should not—not shunt.

Let me—not lemme.

What's your name—not whachna.

Can't you call back—not canchacaba.

Give me—not gimme.

For instance—not frinsance.

Do you know—not dyano.

He's not in—not heznotn.

There's no answer—not thersnoansa.

SUPPORTING TECHNIQUE 4: Plosive Sounds

Plosive sounds are eight of the most important sounds in English for controlling sloppy speech on the phone. Plosives get their name from the necessary buildup of air pressure in the mouth before the sound is made; the articulation of the sound comes as the air pressure is released. The eight plosive sounds are:

b as in boy

d as in dog

g as in girl

j as in jump

p as in put

t as in toy

k as in kite

ch as in child

The difficulty with these sounds on the phone arises when speakers fail to produce them in certain words. They expect listeners on the other end of the phone to fill in the missing sounds. For instance:

wh	instead of white
bla	instead of black
projec	instead of project
ei	instead of eight
comny	instead of company

■ Try This

Practice the following exercise to increase your sensitivity to speaking more clearly on the phone. Read the following sentences aloud, overemphasizing and exploding each plosive sound. You may feel strange and self-conscious saying these sentences. The payoff of speaking clearly, however, will be well worth the effort. Practice with a tape recorder. Underline each plosive sound you omitted as you replay your recording, and then repeat this exercise.

3

1. Pat took the note and left it on the desk.
2. Bob took Ted out to the back of the big white tent.
3. You must speak right into the black mike.
4. The receptionist answered her phone late into the night.
5. Bob will meet with the group and get the most work completed by midnight.
6. Right about eight, the gate will be locked and guarded for the rest of the night.
7. The light is so bright that I can't find the plug or the cord.
8. If your rate is fast, it will be difficult to get what you said.

SUPPORTING TECHNIQUE 5: Rate

Rate refers to the actual number of words a speaker says in one minute. Normal conversation produces approximately 125 to 150 words per minute. A business presentation normally produces 175 to 190 words per minute. Service delivered over the telephone requires much greater flexibility. Your rate of speaking depends on factors such as the quality and clarity of the phone connection, the complexity of the topic, and your own speaking skill.

■ Try This

Practice controlling your rate by reading this paragraph into an answering machine or tape recorder. Play it back to decide how you like it. Try it again a little faster, then again a little more slowly. This will help you get the feel for your rate of speaking. This paragraph contains 176 words. Try to read it in one minute.

> As the report progressed, it became clear that keeping on schedule would be directly related to the ability of the project manager to communicate with the client. Originally, it was thought that weekly meetings would suffice. It quickly became evident that daily communication would be necessary in the later stages of the work. However, travel and distance, unforeseen complications, cost, and even personality emerged as modifying variables. Personality and the individual differences in communication style became key stumbling blocks to the project's progress. The project manager preferred to make a quick phone call and relate the overall progress for the day. The client preferred a more detailed report of specific aspects of the daily tasks. These differences in communication style caused irritations and misunderstandings. These often led to indecision and delay, which created havoc with the schedule and increased the budget. Eventually, it was decided that both the project manager and the client would allow their "next-in-charge" to handle the daily discussions. They got along fine and the project was finished within the budget.

SUPPORTING TECHNIQUE 6: Pace

Pace refers to the length of time a speaker pauses between ideas or thoughts. Pace concerns both how many different topics you should bring to the call and how quickly you should introduce those topics. Without visual cues, delivery of service over the phone requires a greater sensitivity to how much and how fast you can cover information. Whether you are taking information as simple as name, address, and phone number or giving information as complex as chemical formulas or processing codes, the following guidelines will help you control the pace at which you provide service to callers.

When covering	Pause approximately
Very familiar topics	:01 second
Familiar topics	:02 seconds
New topics	:03 seconds
Very new topics	:04 seconds

SUPPORTING TECHNIQUE 7: Inflection

Inflection is the stress or emphasis that a speaker places on a particular word or phrase to enhance meaning. Again, without the benefit of seeing the caller to whom you are providing service, you must be extra aware of the inflection of your messages. Basically, you have three choices:

1. Up inflection implies a question or uncertainty.
2. Straight inflection implies a statement of fact.
3. Down inflection implies an emphatic attitude.

Many speakers accompany a particular inflection pattern with a facial expression or other body gesture to clarify or reinforce the point being made. It is certainly helpful to continue these actions when you are serving a caller. But pay attention to the most appropriate vocal inflection because of the lack of visual contact.

Try This

Tape yourself or record your voice on your answering machine saying these sentences. Notice the differences in inflection and meaning. Try to use the inflection and meaning given in parentheses after each sentence.

1. Good speech is good business. (straight—factual)
2. Mixed messages can cost more than money. (down—emphatic)
3. Phone service can be either good or bad. (up—question)
4. Callers require immediate service. (down—emphatic)
5. I can control the impression I make. (up—question)

LEARNING ACTION PLAN

Use this form to commit to learning and practicing telephone customer service skills. In the middle column, jot down the steps you plan to take to master the skills presented. Set a date for completion of these steps.

LEARNING ACTION PLAN		
Technique	**Action to Take**	**Date Due**
1. Voice	_____	
2. Articulation	_____	
3. Assimilation	_____	
4. Plosive sounds	_____	
5. Rate	_____	
6. Pace	_____	
7. Inflection	_____	

Chapter 3 Checkpoints

✓ Control the sound of your speech and voice carefully.

✓ Practice articulation exercises regularly.

✓ Practice on your answering machine or tape recorder.

✓ Practice out loud.

✓ Speak loudly and clearly enough to be heard 10 feet away.

✓ Do not let your speaking rate and pace make the caller feel uncomfortable.

✓ Don't practice silently.

✓ Don't rush through the articulation exercises.

4 | Listening for Service

This chapter will help you to:

- Understand the difference between hearing callers and listening to callers.
- Understand the importance of listening when serving callers.
- Learn eight supporting techniques for strengthening your listening effectiveness.

I've said it twice already, aren't you listening Rick?

Don't you people listen to what your customers say?

Listen carefully Rick, I'm only going to say this once.

Somebody wasn't listening. This order is wrong again. ■

How many times have you heard these words? Perhaps you've said them. Many callers believe that the root of their problem is the poor listening skills of service providers. Most professional service providers are aware of the importance of good speaking skills. Few are as conscientious about good listening skills.

Let's begin by differentiating between hearing and listening. Hearing and listening are not the same thing. *Hearing* is:

- The physical act of sound striking the eardrum.
- An involuntary and reflexive act.

4

Listening is:

- Differentiating among these sounds.
- A voluntary and interactive act.

Hearing and listening are critical to providing quality phone service. Your ability to *listen* and evaluate while serving your caller may depend on your ability to *hear* the caller. The quality of the connection and the noise around you are only two of the factors that may affect your ability to hear the caller.

Generally speaking, listening can be either active or passive. *Active listening* gives full attention to the caller. *Passive listening* does not give full attention to the caller. The techniques in this chapter are designed to improve active listening.

SUPPORTING TECHNIQUE 1: Be Ready to Listen

Although this sounds simple, it isn't. When you receive a call, you must get physically and psychologically ready to listen. You should have note-taking materials available. You may need to turn off other distractions such as a radio or loud machinery.

Try This

1. Clear your work space of materials not needed to provide immediate service to callers.
2. Be prepared with appropriate forms, notepads, colored pens and pencils, and any technical materials such as tables, charts, and directories. Have these items within arm's reach.
3. When possible, turn your chair and table away from distractions.
4. Close your eyes and listen to the sounds around you. Is anything attracting your attention? It may also distract your attention during a service call.

5. You may need a "do not disturb" note on your door or at your desk to alert others that you are busy.

6. Sit or stand comfortably in a position that promotes efficiency.

Make a commitment to active listening.

SUPPORTING TECHNIQUE 2: Pay Attention

Again, this sounds so simple. But once again it is not. It is easy to be distracted by someone else in the room, by an unusual activity nearby, even by a photograph on the wall. To pay attention means to concentrate on the caller's wants and needs. Avoid daydreaming. You must make an agreement with yourself *not* to think about anything but providing service to the caller during the call.

4

■ Try This

The following hints will help you pay attention to your caller:

1. Differentiate between your caller's service wants and service needs. (Refer back to Chapter 1.)
2. Be objective, not subjective, about the value of your caller's request.
3. Constantly reinforce your understanding of the differences between personal and professional attitudes and behavior.
4. Do not write notes, read memos, or do other work during a service call.

SUPPORTING TECHNIQUE 3: Don't Interrupt

Learn to wait when listening to your caller. Don't finish the caller's sentences, thoughts, or concerns. As a person providing service, you may hear the same concern expressed many times. But for the person needing service, that concern is of utmost importance. Listen, be patient, and don't interrupt.

■ Hints

1. During your next personal conversation with a friend, purposely refrain from responding and offering your opinion. Force yourself not to respond to your friend's opinions until he or she has stopped talking completely.
2. Observe a conversation among a group of people. Note carefully the number and nature of interruptions.
3. Watch and listen to a television news interview program such as "Nightline." Note the attentiveness of the host and the lack of interruptions.

SUPPORTING TECHNIQUE 4: Control Biases

This technique may be the most difficult to master. We all have biases. As a service professional, you need to be aware of your own. For example, you may have biases regarding people with high-pitched voices, an accent, or poor grammar. You may have biases regarding race or religion, or about people who come from a particular region of the country, or section of town.

To control your personal biases, take these steps:

1. Be honest with yourself. Identify your biases regarding people, places, and things.
2. Recognize that bias is a natural part of life. Biases are inherently not bad.
3. Realize that as a service professional, you must not permit your personal biases to affect your professional behavior. Make sure you control, rather than act on, your biases.

SUPPORTING TECHNIQUE 5: Pick Up Cue Words

Cue words are words or phrases callers use that give you clues to their wants and needs. These words and phrases can be particular to an individual, a company, or a culture. Following is a list of common cue words callers use. Understanding them will simplify and strengthen your ability to provide good service.

Cue Word	Common Meaning
Bottom line *"What's the bottom line here?"*	Final decision, cost
Run it by *"I have to run it by my boss."*	Get approval

(continued)

Cue Word	Common Meaning
Rat hole	Line of pursuit with no value
"That sounds like a rat hole we can't afford to get into."	
Blow it up	Expand your ideas
"Blow it up and send me the complete proposal."	
In the ballpark	Within possibility
"Your prices are not in the ballpark."	
Ducks in a row	Everyone's in agreement
"We have our ducks in a row and can begin tomorrow."	
In the pipeline	Making way through the system
"Everything you suggested was already in the pipeline."	
On board	In agreement
"We're glad you're on board with us."	
Ramp up	Preparation time
"There's a six-month ramp up period."	

■ Try This

1. Listen to a conversation among a group of people. List the cue words you hear.

   _____

   _____

2. Listen to your own language in your next professional call. What cue words do you use?

   _____

   _____

3. With your co-workers, create a list of common cue words your callers use. Are there some cues you all hear regularly?

   _____

   _____

SUPPORTING TECHNIQUE 6: Paraphrase

Paraphrasing is repeating the caller's thoughts in your own words. (*Parroting* is repeating the caller's thoughts using the caller's exact words.) When you paraphrase correctly, your caller will know you are a good listener. In addition, you will receive an instant check on the accuracy of what you heard.

■ Try This

1. Periodically repeat what you understood the caller to have said.
2. Use your own words. Don't attempt to repeat every detail.
3. Do not paraphrase every statement the caller has made—only those containing information pertinent to the service.

SUPPORTING TECHNIQUE 7: Separate Fact and Feeling

Appropriate professional service requires that you satisfy both the factual, technical needs and the emotional and nontechnical needs of your caller.

Here is a typical caller's comment that requires you to separate fact and feeling. Can you identify each?

This is the second time I've called and I'm getting annoyed. You only delivered 8 of the 10 boxes in our order, which is upsetting enough. Our contract calls for complete delivery by the 10th. Today is the 15th and it still hasn't arrived. I can't complete this project without better service.

This is the second time I've called [fact] and I'm getting annoyed [feeling]. You only delivered 8 of the 10 boxes in our order [fact], which is upsetting enough [feeling]. Our contract calls for complete delivery by the 10th [fact]. Today is the 15th and it still hasn't arrived [fact]. I can't complete this project without better service [fact].

4

■ **Try This**

1. Tell the caller you would like to understand both the facts and the feelings required for appropriate service.
2. Listen for fact or feeling cue words.
3. Understand the precise requirements of your caller.
4. Before taking calls, identify both the factual and emotional resources available to you.

SUPPORTING TECHNIQUE 8: Be Reassuring

Callers need to know that their requests and opinions will be taken seriously. Being reassuring will help you create the appropriate environment of cooperation and concern.

■ **Try This**

1. Thank the caller for calling.
2. Offer assistance immediately by saying something like "How may I help you?"
3. Use appropriate inflection, speed, pitch, and volume to create the sound of cooperation and concern. (Refer back to Chapter 3.)
4. During a call, periodically use words and phrases such as "I see," "I understand," "Uh huh," "Hmmm," "Sure," and "OK."

LEARNING ACTION PLAN

Use this form to commit to learning and practicing telephone customer service skills. In the middle column, jot down the steps you plan to take to master the skills presented. Set a date for completion of these steps.

LEARNING ACTION PLAN		
Technique	**Action to Take**	**Date Due**
1. Get ready to listen		
2. Pay attention		
3. Don't interrupt		
4. Control biases		
5. Pick up cue words		
6. Paraphrase		
7. Separate fact from feeling		
8. Be reassuring		

Chapter 4 Checkpoints

✓ Be an active listener.

✓ Be physically and mentally prepared to listen.

✓ Control your biases.

✓ Be patient.

✓ Don't interrupt your callers.

5 | The Language of Service

This chapter will help you to:

- Understand the effect of language on service.
- Use language as a tool for strengthening service delivered over the phone.
- Learn the seven Cs of language to be used during phone service calls.
- Develop and refine your personable phone service style.

You stupid old boy! I told you the last time you called to have your account number ready. What's the matter with you? Get with the program, will you? You'll just have to wait until I can look it up. Hold on. ■

You wouldn't use this kind of language with your callers, would you? Of course not! Yes, you may feel like using it, but most service providers have enough control to avoid this obviously bad behavior. Unfortunately, many service providers do use language that conveys a lack of sensitivity and caring.

For example, "Hi, how are you?" is actually a question expressing an interest in your caller's well-being. Too many service providers ask this question and then quickly move on to their own purposes without giving the caller an opportunity to respond.

This chapter focuses on the choice of language and expression used during service calls. Before reading the chapter, think about the words you use in your day-to-day service calls. Use the techniques in the chapter to strengthen your effectivenes in this easy-to-overlook area.

Experts estimate that there are more than 500,000 words in the English language. That presents you with a wide variety of options when you choose the language to use in serving your callers. Some service calls require that you use specific, technical language whereas others require the use of "shirtsleeve," or less formal, English.

Providing service over the phone is easier if you keep your word choice and language construction simple and direct. This does not mean that you must be cold or insensitive. The ideal style for service over the phone is a *personable* style in which you couple carefully chosen language with equally careful use of friendly, caring inflection, speed, and articulation. (Be sure to reread Chapter 3.) This chapter describes the "seven Cs" of personable phone service.

SUPPORTING TECHNIQUE 1: Be Courteous

Being courteous is simple. Use "please" and "thank you" whenever appropriate, which may be several times throughout your call. Also ask permission to speak when you initiate the call—you may be calling at an inconvenient time. Thank the person for giving you his or her time and assistance when you conclude the call. Whenever possible, use the person's name. Do not "sir" and "ma'am" people—it often sounds cold and rude. These words are often used with an "up" inflection or said very quickly. This can create an almost nasty impression.

Replace commonly used language on the left with the courteous alternatives shown on the right.

NOT COURTEOUS	COURTEOUS
You'll have to.	Would you mind? May I ask you to?
I can't.	I'm sorry, I'm unable to.

NOT COURTEOUS	COURTEOUS
I need you to.	May I ask you to?
What's your problem?	Would you mind reviewing the situation?
	May I ask you to explain the circumstances?
You don't understand.	I'm sorry if I'm not being clear.

SUPPORTING TECHNIQUE 2: Be Clear

Keep it short and simple. Use familiar, everyday words. Construct simple declarative sentences. The person on the other end of the phone line may not be giving you full attention or may be distracted unexpectedly. The clarity of your language will help the process, especially when covering technical issues. Do no use tentative language. Here are a few examples:

Not Clear	Clear
I think.	I know.
I hope.	I'm certain.
I feel.	I believe.
It should.	It will.
Probably.	It is.

Try This

1. Identify specific opportunities in your own phone interactions where courteous language would be helpful. Prepare a list of courteous phrases below—be ready to use them.

_____

_____

_____

5

2. Tape record yourself providing information to a caller. Did you use tentative language? How could you clarify and strengthen your use of language?

_____

_____

_____

3. Call a competitor of yours and ask for product or service information. Was the service provider clear? Why or why not?

_____

_____

_____

5

SUPPORTING TECHNIQUE 3: Be Colorful

Your caller cannot see your body language, your smile, or your eyes. Therefore, it is important to make the sound of your voice colorful by using speech, voice, and language tools to create an impression and enhance your meaning. There are three ways to colorize your words when conveying a message, even if the information is very straightforward, black-and-white, and factual.

Important meaning and emphasis can be conveyed by the way you colorize words.

Try This

1. Volume.   Raise or lower your volume on certain words to emphasize a point. In the example below, raising your voice on the word *delighted* places emphasis on a word expressing emotion. This makes the caller feel comfortable.

Not colorful: I'm delighted you called. (All words on same plane.)

Colorful: I'm delighted you called. (Raise voice slightly.)

2. Speed.   Say certain words or phrases faster or slower to express meaning. The following example slows down the word *so*. This technique for controlling speed is called *duration*.

> *Not colorful: Thank you so much for calling.*
> *(All sounds at same speed.)*

> *Colorful: Thank you sooo much for calling.*
> *(Prolonged sound.)*

3. Inflection.   Raise or lower your inflection on specific words to express meaning. This is most useful in showing empathy, caring, and concern.

> *Not colorful: That's such a shame.*
> *(A monopattern throughout sentence.)*

> *Colorful: That's* such *a* shame.
> *(Upward inflection on* such *and* shame.*)*

■ **Hints** ─────────────────────────────

Practice using more colorful language in your next call. Chances are, you'll notice a more animated and engaged response from your client or customer.

SUPPORTING TECHNIQUE 4: Be Concise

Too often callers are at the mercy of long, complex phone conversations. By the time they get a response to their questions or inquiries, they may have forgotten the original need or concern. You probably hear colleagues using inconcise language frequently. Are there ways to help them be more concise? Be concise to avoid this problem.

> *Not concise: I want to thank you for calling and letting me know that your computer has broken down and you are unable to use it so you cannot ask your staff to word process your letters and this holds you up and slows down your business which in turn . . . and on and on.*

Concise: Thank you for calling and informing me of your computer break-down. I will arrange a service call immediately.

SUPPORTING TECHNIQUE 5: Be Consistent

Being consistent when providing service to a caller is necessary to avoid confusion. When you repeatedly refer to a product, idea, service, or individual, keep the identifying labels and terms the same throughout the conversation. Too often the mistake of changing names, titles, or terminology causes confusion, leading to poor caller service.

5

Not consistent: I will notify the supervisor that your printer has been having problems and has been distorting your letters. The manager will inform me who repairs laser writers when they don't print clear letters.

Consistent: I will be happy to notify the supervisor responsible for repairing laser printers and specify your problem as letter distortion.

Hints

Make a vocabulary list of the many different ways you refer to your products and services. Choose a specific consistent set of terms to describe your product or service and purposely use only those words in your next service call.

SUPPORTING TECHNIQUE 6: Be Correct

In providing service to callers, slang and profanity are neither correct nor effective. You must be certain you are using correct pronunciation, grammar, and word choice. The most effective language is grammatically correct language. Here are a few examples that illustrate the most common errors.

Incorrect: Like, it's one of the best products we have.
Correct: It's one of the best products we have.

Incorrect: She sounds like she's pleased with your service.
Correct: She sounds as if she's pleased with your service.

Incorrect: I've had about 50 calls today from our ad in the paper.
Correct: I've had 46 calls today because of our ad in the paper.

A few of the most frequently mispronounced words are shown in the left hand column below. Be sure to practice the correct pronunciation in all the professional calls you make.

Incorrect	**Correct**
Nucular	Nukleear
Aks	Ask
Lenth	Length
Libary	Library
Tetnichal	Technical
Recunize	Recognize
Probly	Probably
Picher	Picture (Pic cher)

SUPPORTING TECHNIQUE 7: Be Communicative

You must be able to comfortably communicate with your customer or client. In telephone service, that means, *talk!* Talk to your caller. Although it is important to be to the point and expeditious in your service manner, it is also important to be personable. Being communicative does not mean talking about just anything. It means talking about the concerns and issues that are the purpose of the call. Every caller should be made to feel like a VIP (very important person). In fact, that's the name of a popular technique: the VIP technique.

VIP

1. **Be vocal.** Be the first to speak. Use an appropriate greeting or comment. Don't wait for the caller.

2. **Be informative.** Supply your caller with information about who you are, what you can and will do, and what the caller can do.

3. **Be personable.** Use open-ended questions rather than close-ended questions.

Being communicative and personable are key skills in providing excellent customer and client service.

LEARNING ACTION PLAN

Use this form to commit to learning and practicing telephone customer service skills. In the middle column, jot down the steps you plan to take to master the skills presented. Set a date for completion of these steps.

LEARNING ACTION PLAN		
Technique	**Action to Take**	**Date Due**
1. Be courteous		
2. Be clear		
3. Be colorful		
4. Be concise		
5. Be consistent		
6. Be correct		
7. Be communicative		

Chapter 5 Checkpoints

✓ Practice the seven Cs of telephone service.

✓ Be personable with your callers.

✓ Use appropriate language.

✓ Practice the VIP technique.

✓ Do not use slang or profanity with callers.

✓ Do not be verbose or curt.

✓ Check your language by regularly tape recording it.

6 | Controlling the Process

This chapter will help you to:

- Make and take calls.
- Control the process of handling calls.
- Begin and end calls.
- Make and take messages effectively.
- Handle the hold button.

Hi, Kelly, welcome to your new job.

Hi, Ethan, thanks. What do I do first?

Oh, it's easy. Just answer the calls that come in.

Well, what do I say, and who's calling anyway?

Nobody important, only customers. All you have to do is answer their questions, maybe take a message, and sometimes call them back. It's easy.

Well, Ethan, is there any training needed?

Na, it's easy, just talk to them. ■

▪ Questions to Consider

1. What went wrong here?

   _____

   _____

   _____

2. Do you have problems like this in your organization?

_____

_____

_____

Providing service by phone is a process with identifiable skills that can be improved. Some businesses may require a few additional steps in the process unique to that business. Whether making or taking calls, almost every business utilizes the steps in the process identified here. As a service professional, your skill in controlling these steps is directly tied to the ultimate satisfaction of yourself and your customer or client.

SUPPORTING TECHNIQUE 1: Attitude

Controlling your attitude, as has been made clear already, is critical for success in providing service to callers on the telephone. One of the most important things to remember about controlling your attitude about service calls is that every call is an opportunity, not an interruption!

Try This

1. Identify the times of day, people, or events that affect your mood and be prepared to control and communicate accordingly.

_____

_____

_____

2. Randomly call two or three service companies. What attitude is communicated by the phone service you receive?

_____

_____

_____

3. Call your own company and evaluate its attitude.

_____

_____

_____

SUPPORTING TECHNIQUE 2: Be Prepared

As discussed in Chapter 4, make sure you have the materials that you need to control calls—simple materials such as pens, pencils, pads, forms, directories, files, and lists—within arm's reach. Know the purpose of your call, if you are making the call. If you are taking calls, know your role and know your caller's expectations. Remember, you are expected to at least meet, and if possible to exceed, those expectations with the sound of superior service.

■ Hints

1. Make a list of the necessary materials you need to be fully prepared to provide service to callers.
2. Gather these materials around you within arm's reach and practice reaching them, turning pages, using a computer, and so on.

6

SUPPORTING TECHNIQUE 3: Beginning the Call

Similar skills should be used in making and taking calls. There are four steps in making calls, and four similar steps in taking calls.

■ Try This

Follow the steps on page 56 to prepare an effective way to open professional calls that you make or receive. There is a slight but important difference between making and taking calls. Read the following scripts carefully.

Making Calls

1. Greeting.   "Good morning."
2. Identify self.   "This is Dylan Murphy calling."
3. Identify company.   "From Tampa Family Services."
4. State purpose.   "May I speak to Rick please."

Taking Calls

1. Greeting.   "Good morning."
2. Identify company.   "Tampa Family Company."
3. Identify self.   "This is Dylan."
4. Offer assistance.   "How may I help you?"

1. Write out an appropriate beginning for making a call. Include your company's preferred method of introducing itself, your purpose for calling, and an appropriate, courteous greeting.

_____
_____
_____
_____

2. Write out an appropriate beginning for taking a call. Include your company's preferred method of identification, and announce your willingness to be of service.

_____
_____
_____
_____

3. Practice each of these openings with appropriate, upbeat, and friendly inflection and style.

4. To help ensure complete control of your sound of service, practice saying your beginning comments five times fast. Now, slow your beginning down to normal speed and notice your greater control and flexibility.

SUPPORTING TECHNIQUE 4:
Keep the Call Moving

During most calls there are common events that you should be able to handle in a professional, proficient, courteous, and personable manner.

1. Putting People on Hold.   The hold button is not a weapon. Do not use it to put an obnoxious, annoying, or irritating caller into the never-never land of hold. In fact, if you can avoid putting people on hold, do so. Being placed on hold may create unpleasant and unproductive feelings—no one likes it. Callers understand that hold is important and perhaps inevitable, however, and they appreciate hearing that you are sensitive to their impatience. Putting people on hold is an opportunity to make a professional and personable impression.

- Ask callers if they mind being placed on hold.
- Tell them why they will be on hold.
- Estimate the time they will be on hold.
- Thank them and then put them on hold.
- When you return from hold, thank them.
- Let them know that you understand how difficult it is to hold.
- Soften the experience by such tools as music, a local radio station, or special tapes devised for people on hold. Avoid jokes on hold; they upset people more because they may be cut off just before the punch line.

2. Taking Messages.   You surely appreciate it when your colleagues take messages that are thorough and clear. You should be equally conscientious when taking messages for the sake of both the party receiving and the party leaving the message. See page 58 for an example of a clear message.

- Write down information as you get it. Don't depend on your memory.
- Get the name and phone number and all pertinent facts and information. Ask for correct spelling of all names, titles, and so on.

- Don't use jargon or abbreviations that may be misunderstood later.
- Repeat the message to the person you are speaking with.
- Whenever necessary and possible, write names and unusual terms phonetically in parentheses (par-ren-tha-sees). This will help others pronounce these words clearly later on.

A MESSAGE FOR: *Sheila Liberman*

FROM *Carla Tishler*   DATE *1/18/94*

OF *Mirror Copy Shop*   TIME *1:30* ~~AM~~ (PM)

PHONE No. *617-964-5508*   FAX _____

☐ TELEPHONED   ☑ PLEASE CALL
☐ CAME TO SEE YOU   ☐ WANTS TO SEE YOU
☑ RETURNED YOUR CALL   ☐ WILL CALL AGAIN

MESSAGE *How many copies of the Phoenix report do you want?*

CALL TAKEN BY *Heather Pickford*

---

3. Giving Messages. Your message will be delivered more clearly and accurately if you help the message taker by doing a few simple things:

- Have a clear idea of what you want to leave as a message.
- Ask the other person to kindly write the information down.
- Use short simple sentences when conveying your message.
- Spell all names, titles, streets, and the like to ensure accuracy.
- Ask the message taker to repeat the message information.
- Ask for the name of the message taker.
- Thank the person by name for his or her assistance.

SUPPORTING TECHNIQUE 5: Ending the Call

Many people seem to be impressed only by the last or latest contact they have had with you, and they remember the way you ended the call more than the way you handled the rest of the process. So don't get careless in the closing moments. The ending, like the beginning, of a call has four elements: a thank you, repetition of the caller's name, final confirmation, and a final salutation. Be sure to include all four:

Thank you.	Thanks for giving me this time.
Caller's name.	Mr. Stefan.
Final confirmation.	I'll put those materials in the mail today.
Final salutation.	Good bye.

You may vary these words, of course, but be certain to cover all four elements. Follow the steps below to set up appropriate endings for phone calls.

6

■ Try This

1. Write out an appropriate ending for making a call. Include a thank you, the caller's name, final confirmation, and a final salutation.

   _____

   _____

   _____

   _____

2. Write out an appropriate ending for taking a call. Include the same elements in question 1 above.

   _____

   _____

   _____

   _____

3. Practice each of these endings with appropriate, upbeat, and friendly inflection and style.

4. To help ensure complete control of your sound of service, practice saying your ending comments five times fast. Now, slow down to normal speed and notice your greater control and flexibility.

LEARNING ACTION PLAN

Use this form to commit to learning and practicing telephone customer service skills. In the middle column, jot down the steps you plan to take to master the skills presented. Set a date for completion of these steps.

LEARNING ACTION PLAN		
Technique	**Action to Take**	**Date Due**
1. Attitude		
2. Be prepared		
3. Beginning the call		
4. Keep the call moving		
5. Ending the call		

Chapter 6 Checkpoints

✓ Control the calling process.

✓ Practice a personalized, appropriate beginning and ending for each call.

✓ Practice your personable phone style.

✓ Do not treat any caller casually.

✓ Do not use the hold button as a weapon.

7 | Handling Upset Callers and Other Problems

This chapter will help you to:

- Provide effective service to *all* callers.
- Learn a method for handling service complaints.
- Use a six-step problem-solving format.

Listen Monica, just do what you're hired to do. Get me that information. I don't do business with you people so I can hear your bellyaching and excuses about your lousy ability to do your job. If you can't handle this, stop your whining and connect me with someone who can. ■

■ Questions to Consider

1. Have you had to deal with this kind of caller?

_____

_____

_____

2. How do you handle these kinds of calls?

_____

_____

_____

No service provider likes to hear anger and abuse over the phone. In this chapter, you will learn how to handle these kinds of situations.

When providing service over the phone, you will occasionally meet callers who are angry or distraught. Their anger may be caused by matters totally unrelated to you, your company, your products, or your service. People often find it easy to vent their emotions on a nonpersonal voice at the other end of the phone. Somehow, they relate their personal upset to the service call. Your job, as a service professional, is to separate the facts from feelings and provide effective, efficient responses without becoming emotionally involved. Here are several supporting techniques that will help you develop the skills necessary to provide comfortable service to customers and clients over the phone.

SUPPORTING TECHNIQUE 1: The F-F-F Method

F-F-F is a long-standing technique for helping control callers who are very upset. It can be used in virtually any business setting. You should perform the technique in the appropriate order, but you may vary the language according to your needs. It is important, however, to perform this technique in the order shown. Following is an illustration of F-F-F applied to an upset caller.

Do you realize we waited three days for this delivery? A full crew of technicians sat around with nothing to do waiting for your inept delivery system to do what you promised. I'm angry! I plan to report this stupidity to the proper authorities.

1st F: Feel.   You must understand how the caller feels ("I understand how you feel"). This may be the most critical part of the entire technique. The words should not be spoken—in fact, no words should be spoken—until your caller has completely finished telling you about his concern. This may be particularly difficult for you. As a service professional, you may have heard this service concern expressed many times. You may actually be able to resolve the concern very quickly. However, your caller is experiencing that concern in a personal way—perhaps for the first time. Do not interrupt him. When the caller has finished expressing his feelings, then convey your feeling:

I understand how you feel. It's very upsetting when you don't get the service you expect.

2nd F: Felt.   Convey to the caller that you have felt the way he feels yourself ("I have felt that way myself"). Say so immediately after the first F and follow with a personal anecdote explaining *why* and *how* you have felt the same way. It is critical that you relay this personal anecdote in less than 10 seconds. Your caller does not want to listen to your problems.

> *I've* felt *the same way when I waited home all day for the telephone repair crew to show up. It wasted my whole day. I understand your feeling of frustration.*

3rd F: Found.   Convey to the caller that you have found a solution to his problem ("I have found that the best thing to do is . . ."). At this point, you must provide the caller with at least one, and preferably several, options for resolution.

> *I have* found *that the best thing to do is call the local delivery vendor right away. I'll take care of that. Next we must recheck the specified delivery arrangements. You check that end and I'll check this end. I will also ask my boss for special permission to deliver new materials overnight if we cannot locate them. I'll arrange confirmation calls one week prior to future deliveries.*

7

■ Hints

1. Use F-F-F in a nonbusiness situation such as deciding on a location for dinner or negotiating vacation plans.
2. Using three different colored markers, write F-F-F in two-inch letters on a postcard. Tape the postcard to the edge of your telephone as a reminder.
3. Make F-F-F a normal part of your call reponse routine.

SUPPORTING TECHNIQUE 2:
Handling Complaints

This technique is helpful when callers have a specific complaint or complaints regarding your product or service. It will help you isolate objections and enable you to deal with them more efficiently. It is important that you practice the technique in this order:

1. **Hear the complaint.** Allow callers to relate their concerns completely before you move to the next step.

2. **Question the complaint.** Begin by asking callers "May I ask you a few questions?" This will indicate that you are interested in their concerns. It will also provide callers with a sense of control. Ask whatever clarifying questions are helpful.

3. **Confirm the information.** Repeat the salient facts and feelings. This will reassure the caller of your concern and accuracy.

4. **Answer the complaint.** Provide the appropriate service response. This, of course, will vary according to the request, the complaint, and your company's policies.

5. **Confirm your answer.** Review the concerns identified earlier and be sure both you and the caller agree you have answered those concerns.

6. **Ask for agreement.** Ask the caller to agree that the complaint has been satisfactorily resolved.

H i n t s

1. Post the above six-step technique by your telephone where you can easily see it.
2. Make this technique part of your call response routine.

SUPPORTING TECHNIQUE 3:
Six-Step Problem Solving

This technique is helpful when callers have a nonspecific concern but need to resolve a problem.

1. Identify the Problem.   Allow and encourage callers to describe the problem in their own terminology. Do not interrupt while they are doing so. Conclude this step by constructing a question that details the caller's request.

2. Define the Terms.   Offer specific definitions of terms used in stating the problem. Your understanding of a simple description such as *all day*

The Six-Step Problem Solving Format

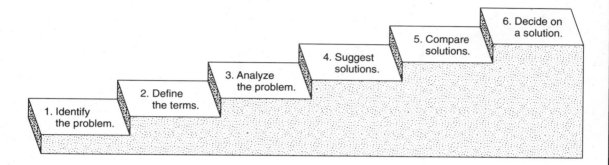

may be very different from the caller's. Don't assume you both mean the same thing by using the same language. Offer a specific definition and make sure your caller agrees before moving on.

3. Analyze the Problem.   Review the facts of the problem, including who, when, what, where, and how.

4. Suggest Solutions.   Based on the information you gather in the three preceding steps, suggest two or three reasonable solutions. In fact, ask callers to suggest a reasonable solution or two of their own.

5. Compare Solutions.   Objectively compare and contrast the advantages and disadvantages of each solution suggested.

6. Decide on a Solution.   Carefully select the most appropriate, efficient, and effective solution.

Hints ———————————————————————

1. Use this six-step problem-solving format the next time you are deciding on a car to buy.

2. Copy these six steps onto a card you can post near your phone where you can see it easily.

3. Make this technique a normal part of your call response routine.

LEARNING ACTION PLAN

Use this form to commit to learning and practicing telephone customer service skills. In the middle column, jot down the steps you plan to take to master the skills presented. Set a date for completion of these steps.

LEARNING ACTION PLAN		
Technique	**Action to Take**	**Date Due**
1. F-F-F Method	_____ _____	
2. Handling complaints	_____ _____	
3. Six-step problem solving	_____ _____	

Chapter 7 Checkpoints

✓ Have patience with callers who complain.

✓ Use your best listening skills and techniques.

✓ Separate personal and professional attitudes and behaviors.

✓ Don't interrupt callers when they are complaining.

✓ Don't jump to conclusions regarding complaints.

✓ Be a problem-solving partner with your customer or client.

8 | Controlling "Phonephobia"

This chapter will help you to:

- Understand the psychological and physiological elements of phone service anxiety.
- Learn four techniques for controlling phone service anxiety.
- Understand the importance of the breathing process and its effects on your phone voice.
- Understand how posture controls your phone voice.
- Use the 10-second relaxer.

I didn't go into this line of work so that I could spend my time on the phone with customers. In fact, I hate that part of my job. I don't like talking on the phone. It actually makes me nervous, and I know they can hear it on the other end. I just don't like the phone. ∎

It may seem hard to believe, but some phone service professionals actually suffer from "phonephobia." Phonephobia is not exactly fear of the phone; it is more of a discomfort in using the phone or a dislike of speaking with people over the phone. Phonephobia produces uncomfortable, upsetting symptoms that not only feel bad, but also have a negative effect on your ability to provide good service.

Phonephobia causes such things as:

- Sweaty palms.
- Rapid heartbeat.
- Temperature change.

- Upset stomach.
- Shaky voice.
- Inability to concentrate.

Phonephobia may not be pervasive, but it is not uncommon. Why would someone with phonephobia be in the phone service business? You may not have a choice, for example, if your job requires you to provide phone service if you are the technical or product expert, or if, as in many companies, reorganization has given you added responsibilities. Phonephobia or not, you may be required to provide professional phone service.

SUPPORTING TECHNIQUE 1:
Understanding the ABCs

Phonephobics often describe their experience in words like these:

It bothers me when people call me names. That gets me upset.

When I have to place calls to famous people, my voice gets shaky.

Handling important people makes my heart beat faster.

To help control these feelings, use the **A-B-C** technique. **A** stands for the things that *activate* the feelings of anxiety. In our examples these would be:

People calling me names.

Calls to famous people.

Handling important people.

B stands for *beliefs* about the anxiety activators. In our examples these might be:

This embarrasses me. I believe they hate me.

I'm not worthy to talk to them. I believe they think I'm just an adoring fan.

I'm not important to them. I believe they think little of me.

C stands for the *consequences* of such beliefs. In our examples, these would be:

My stomach gets upset.

My voice gets shaky.

My heart beats faster.

Your beliefs are at the root of your anxiety and the consequences you experience. To change the consequences, you must change your beliefs. The uncomfortable consequences of your anxiety are not what activates the anxiety; what you believe activates the anxiety.

■ Try This

1. Identify your **As**. What specific circumstances activate the anxiety? Be specific. You may have a number of **As**.

2. Debate your **Bs**. Conduct a rational debate with yourself over the real and perceived results of each **B** you identify. Be honest with yourself. Ask yourself:
   - Why do you believe this **B**?
   - What started each **B**?
   - What reinforces each **B**?

3. Develop techniques (using this book) to control each **A**.

4. Practice your new techniques until you can actually believe that you are in control of each.

SUPPORTING TECHNIQUE 2: Controlling Diaphragmatic Breathing

Breathing is such a natural, life-sustaining process that most people don't stop to think about its impact on communication. The breathing process plays a critical role in controlling phonephobia. From a jittery stomach to a trembling voice, monitoring your breathing can control it all.

There are three types of breathing:

1. **Clavicular breathing.** This type, which is good for athletes vigorously working out, is a panting, heavy breathing with quick inhalation and exhalation. It is *not* appropriate for controlling phonephobia.

2. **Upper-thoracic breathing.** This breathing is used for any upper-body activity such as lifting, pulling, pushing, and the like. It, too, is *not* appropriate for controlling phonephobia.

3. **Diaphragmatic breathing.** This breathing is designed for the normal inhalation and exhalation process. It is controlled by your diaphragm, which is a large dome-shaped muscle just below your rib cage. This is the body's *natural* method of breathing, and *it is the most appropriate breathing for controlling phonephobia.*

When the symptoms of phonephobia appear, check your breathing. Be able to switch from upper-thoracic breathing to diaphragmatic breathing. Trembling body parts, a shaking voice, and forgetting what you were about to say are all direct results of upper-thoracic breathing, which depletes oxygen in your system and produces unwanted pressure in your body. To practice diaphragmatic breathing, practice the techniques on pages 22–23. As you can see, the same breathing techniques that make you a more confident speaker also ease phone-induced anxiety.

SUPPORTING TECHNIQUE 3:
Controlling Body Position

Stomach in, chest out, don't slouch.

These commands were given to all of us as we grew up. Although seemingly superfluous, they actually are critical to improving your phone service to callers. Your posture affects phone service quality, and good posture helps you eliminate phonephobia. Did you know that:

- Your *larynx* (voice box) is where sound is produced.
- The larynx is located at the top of the trachea (windpipe), behind the Adam's apple.
- The larynx moves from side to side.
- Changing your posture affects the amount of air passing through your larynx.

- Posture affects all other sound resonators such as the pharynx (the space at the back of your throat), nasal passages, sinuses, and oral cavity.
- Poor posture inhibits your diaphragmatic breathing pattern.
- Poor breathing has an impact on the quality of your phone service, both physiologically and psychologically.

Try This

Poor posture can be alleviated by following the steps below.

1. In front of a mirror, practice standing against a wall. The back of your head, shoulders, buttocks, and heels must be against the wall.

2. In front of a mirror, practice sitting naturally with your back against the chair and your feet on the floor. Be sure your buttocks and the heels of your feet line up.

3. Imagine yourself as a rag doll. Let your shoulders relax and slouch forward. Let your head and chin fall forward. Relax your entire body. Let your whole body feel limp and relaxed.

4. Now, slowly tighten up your entire body, from the bottom of your toes to the top of your head. Pull your head, chin, and shoulders erect. Hold this tension for five seconds and release. Repeat steps 3 and 4.

5. In a relaxed position using good posture, practice breathing diaphragmatically, being certain to use your abdominal muscles correctly. Your shoulders and upper chest should not move.

6. Before sitting, stand with your feet 36 inches apart. Rotate your upper body left to right five times.

7. Fully extend your arms away from your body at shoulder length and repeat step 6.

8. Reach high over your head and stretch each arm fully as if trying to touch the ceiling.

8

9. Do five deep knee bends.

10. Stand quietly relaxed and do diaphragmatic breathing for one minute.

SUPPORTING TECHNIQUE 4:
The 10-Second Relaxer

Phonephobia can interfere with providing service to callers during a phone call. A simple, quick technique known as the *10-second relaxer* instantly relieves the physical symptoms of phonephobia. It is particularly helpful when you are not able to use the diaphragmatic breathing technique.

Try This

1. Point your chin toward your chest. You will notice your shoulders and upper chest moving as you use upper-thoracic breathing.

2. Tightly squeeze together the tips of your thumbs and index fingers as you inhale. Increase the pressure at the end of each inhalation.

3. Exhale slowly, releasing tension in the fingers. When the exhalation is complete, your fingers should be separated.

4. Repeat this exercise three times to release the pressure created by upper-thoracic breathing. You can return to diaphragmatic breathing and your voice will remain calm and relaxed.

LEARNING ACTION PLAN

Use this form to commit to learning and practicing telephone customer service skills. In the middle column, jot down the steps you plan to take to master the skills presented. Set a date for completion of these steps.

LEARNING ACTION PLAN		
Technique	**Action to Take**	**Date Due**
1. Understanding the ABCs	_____ _____	
2. Controlling diaphragmatic breathing	_____ _____	
3. Controlling body position	_____ _____	
4. The 10-second relaxer	_____ _____	

Chapter 8 Checkpoints

✓ Phonephobia has two elements: psychological and physiological.

✓ Identify your As.

✓ Challenge your Bs.

✓ Practice diaphragmatic breathing.

✓ Practice posture exercises.

✓ Don't worry before a call.

✓ Don't slouch over when speaking with callers.

✓ Don't breathe upper-thoracically.

9 | Technology

This chapter will help you to:

- Understand the impact of technology on providing telephone service.
- Avoid "voice mail jail."

Stefan, will you and Greg please come in here and explain how this new phone works? It's so annoying—I can't even make a simple call anymore. How the heck does this phone work? What are all these buttons for? Yesterday, it was ringing and ringing and I couldn't even figure out how to answer it. And forget about putting anybody on hold or transferring a call. No way! I'd wind up sending the call to Tibet. Why can't phones be as simple as they always were? ■

■ Questions to Consider

1. Why do you think this person is having difficulty with the phone system?
2. What should this person's organization do to make employees feel comfortable with the phone system?

THE FUTURE IS NOW

Be prepared! Telephone technology is changing as you read these words. Everything from resistors to receivers, from dial tones to satellites, from operators to software is changing rapidly. Perhaps the most significant aspect of this changing technology is the decreased dependence on people to provide phone service. Just a few years ago you could easily predict that a service call would be handled by a person. Today that prediction cannot be made. Although some companies insist on providing the personal touch and ensure that their service calls are always answered by a person, many companies, both large and small, are turning to phone-answering systems that do not require people. Instead, a computer answers calls and in some cases directs callers to a specific department or person. You must be prepared.

There can be no doubt that the technology of providing customer and client service over the phone is changing rapidly. Keep in mind that no matter how sophisticated the technology, callers still come to you one at a time. Each call is placed by a person who has a specific concern. Callers do not rely on sophisticated technology to convey their concern. They pick up the phone and call you. They talk to you. As professional service providers, you must respond in kind. The emerging tools of technology should be no more than tools that assist you in your mission to provide effective personable service over the phone.

Use electronic devices to facilitate your phone service. Use them to control costs. But don't forget to provide the human touch. There is truth in the words "high-tech requires high-touch," as we'll see later in this chapter.

VOICE MAIL

Voice mail—you love it, you hate it, but it's here to stay. Your company probably uses an electronic answering system because it is cost effective.

Put on your customer calling hat for a moment. Have you ever placed a call for service that resulted in a visit to "voice mail jail"? You place a call that is answered by a computer giving you options. You select the desired options, follow the directions, and are greeted by another computer voice giving you more options. You select the desired options. Then you are greeted by another computer voice presenting yet another list of options. You listen, trying to remember the list, the titles, the numbers, the names, and the directions, hoping you haven't forgotten or missed the appropriate selection because if so you will have to return to the very beginning and start all over again. You make your final selection and reach the voice mail of the party or department you're calling, only to hear that the voice mailbox is completely full and you cannot leave a message. *You are in voice mail jail.*

Consider this example:

You have reached the electronic answering service of ACME CONSOLI-DATED. If you are calling from a touch tone phone, press 1 now. If you know your party's extension, you may dial it now. If you do not know your party's extension or require operator assistance, please press hold.

Press 1 Beep
If you are calling to schedule service, press 1.

If you are calling to report a product malfunction, press 2.

If you are calling to request product information, press 3.

Press 2 Beep
If you're calling to report a malfunction of an industrial product, press 1.

If you are calling to report a malfunction of a consumer product, press 2.

If you are calling to report a malfunction that has been previously serviced, press 3.

If you are calling to request emergency service, press 4.

Press 4 Beep
If your product warranty covers emergency service, press 1.

If your product warranty does not cover emergency service, press 2.

If you have been unable to contact your nearest service representative, press 3.

Press 2 Beep
Enter the first three digits of your product ID number.

Enter the five-digit product serial number.

Enter the first two letters of the state where the product is located.

At the tone, enter a detailed description of the product malfunction.

TONE   Beep

We are sorry, the voice mailbox that is dedicated to receive your message is full. Please call back later.

BEEP

SUPPORTING TECHNIQUE 1: Don't Build a Voice Mail Jail

If you have experienced this as a customer caller, you understand the frustration, anger, and anguish that follow. As a phone service professional, one of your most important responsibilities is to avoid constructing a voice mail jail.

The following list will help you to be personable in your efforts to use technology without creating a voice mail jail:

1. Empty voice mailboxes frequently.
2. Be sure the menu options are clear and succinct.
3. Thank callers periodically for their patience and participation in the process.
4. Use your most welcoming and personable voice.
5. Use people's voices rather than computer-generated voices whenever possible.

Hints

Call your company's electronic answering service. Identify and evaluate voice components and develop appropriate recommendations for strengthening your company's welcoming and personable voice.

Be prepared to provide the human sound of service if your company does utilize an electronic phone device. When callers hear your personal prerecorded greeting, make sure they hear the personable sounds of service that say "welcome," "thanks for calling," "nice to hear from you," or "how may I help you."

Be certain that your recorded greeting is:

- Clearly articulated.
- Not assimilated.
- Said at the appropriate rate of speed and pace.
- Not filled with jargon or too technical.

Be sure that you use a friendly voice with a personable style that:

- Has an appropriate mix of up, down, and straight inflection.
- Exercises proper breath support.
- Has a smile in the sound.
- Uses short, simple sentences.
- Requests permission for placing people on hold.
- Is patient.
- Thanks the caller for information.

9

HIGH-TECH REQUIRES HIGH-TOUCH

As these new technologies are used more in telephone customer service, we must make special efforts to personalize and humanize their use. It was never more true that high-tech requires high-touch. What is high-touch? It is a combination of two things. *Understanding* and *action*.

SUPPORTING TECHNIQUE 2: Understanding

High-touch means understanding that callers have wants and needs when they call. We must recognize the differences between these wants and needs (Chapter 1), even though it may not be possible to meet all of them. We must be particularly sensitive to the human needs of each other (Chapter 1). It may be difficult for the caller to understand these, so your role as a service provider takes an even deeper meaning.

Understanding also means the ability to identify *your* human needs. As a service professional you must understand your attitudes, biases, and stressors, and devise a strategy for dealing with them (Chapter 2). Finally, understanding means recognizing the differences between personal and professional styles of communication. It means developing a personable style that bridges these two (Chapter 1).

SUPPORTING TECHNIQUE 3: Action

High-touch means putting into action all of the various human tools and techniques introduced in this book. Such topics as breathing, stress control, diet and fitness, and voice development will all help you be prepared to take the actions necessary for personable phone servicing.

The majority of techniques in this book are aimed at giving you specific actions to take when delivering service over the phone. Coverage of speaking speed (Chapter 3), assimilation and plosives, (Chapter 3), problem solving (Chapter 3), being colorful (Chapter 5), and controlling inflection (Chapter 3) gives you the tools to bring high-touch to your use of high-tech.

Chapter 9 Checkpoints

✓ Be prepared to control technology.

✓ Remember that callers are human.

✓ Provide the human sound of service.

✓ Do not use technology as a weapon.

✓ Do not let technology get in the way of your service skills.

✓ Do not forget the importance of the human touch.

✓ Do not build a voice mail jail.

10 | Putting It All Together

This chapter will help you to:

- Integrate the attitudes and behavior you have learned.
- Refine your personable style.
- Put the sound of welcome in the sound of your service.

If we could give one name to the combined use of the techniques introduced in this book, it would be the Welcome Approach. Perhaps the most important service you can provide to customers and clients over the phone is to help them feel welcome. The skill of helping people feel that you welcome them is invaluable. Each of us appreciates the person who responds to our concerns by helping us feel important. As service professionals, your control of the attitudes and behaviors outlined in this book will convey the all-important feeling of comfort and welcome to each of your callers.

The Welcome Approach carefully combines the actions and insight you bring to each particular service call. Some calls require greater control over the mechanics of speaking clearly. Some calls require greater sensitivity to bias control. Some calls require stellar listening techniques. The efficient selection of appropriate techniques and the effective execution of those techniques are the signs of a company's most valuable service professionals.

THE WELCOME APPROACH

W: Welcome

- Welcome every call as an opportunity, not an interruption.
- Welcome the opportunity to exercise your professional skills.
- Welcome the opportunity to learn how customers and clients feel about your company, product, or service.
- Offer to be of assistance in any situation.
- Say "thank you for calling."
- Use a pleasant greeting.

E: Enthusiasm

- Keep a smile on your face and in your voice.
- Think positively about the helping aspects of your role.
- Sound enthusiastic and energetic over the phone.
- Speak loud enough to be heard by someone sitting 10 feet away.
- Use colorful words whenever appropriate.

L: Listening

- Be a good listener.
- Take notes.
- Ask questions.
- Don't speak longer than 30 seconds without allowing the person on the other end to participate.
- Review periodically.
- Paraphrase important information.
- Don't interrupt.
- Control your biases.

10

C: Courteous

- Say please and thank you when appropriate.
- Use the caller's name whenever possible.
- Respect the caller's right to disagree.
- Ask permission to put the caller on hold.
- Thank callers for remaining on hold.
- Treat callers with respect.

O: Open

- Control your biases.
- Keep a positive attitude.
- Practice the Golden Rule: Do unto others as you would have them do unto you.
- Have patience and tolerance with the shortcomings of others.

Use the welcome approach in all your phone interactions. It works!

10

M: Mechanics

- Refine and practice the sound of service.
- Use clear articulation and pronunciation.
- Control your rate and pace of speaking.
- Avoid tentative and ambiguous language.
- Practice voice, strengthening, and relaxation exercises.
- Be careful of the uncertainty and insincerity that an upward inflection can communicate.

E: Extraordinary

- Meet and exceed the caller's expectations.
- Give everyone special treatment.
- Separate personal attitudes and behaviors from professional attitudes and behaviors.
- Provide options when problem solving.
- Take pride in your professional service skills.
- Understand human behavior, especially the hierarchy of human needs.

Post-Tests

SELF-ASSESSMENTS AND OBSERVER ASSESSMENTS

To determine how well you have incorporated the features of this book into your daily telephone service, go back to the beginning of the book and complete the assessments there again. At this point, the observer assessment is very important. Outside observers should be able to see improvement in the quality of your phone service. If any deficiencies still remain, look back on the chapters that relate most to your weak areas.

MULTIPLE-CHOICE

Circle the letter choices of the best responses.

1. Clients and customers expect
   a. a relationship with you.
   b. direct, efficient, and immediate service.
   c. that you know their name.

2. The most important aspect of delivering professional service is
   a. being on a first-name basis.
   b. being personable.
   c. taking calls any time of the day or the night.

3. Internal customers are those who
   a. work with you.
   b. have connections to your boss.
   c. work indoors.

4. In normal conversation, people produce approximately how many words per minute?

   a. 90–125 words per minute

   b. 125–150 words per minute

   c. 150–200 words per minute

5. When speaking on the telephone, speak loudly and clearly enough to be heard.

   a. 2 feet away.

   b. 5 feet away.

   c. 10 feet away.

6. Make your caller feel like a VIP. This involves being

   a. Verbal, Informative, and Prompt.

   b. Vocal, Informative, and Personable.

   c. Vocal, Interested, and Personable.

7. Your attitude regarding each service call should be

   a. This call is interrupting my work, but I am handling phones.

   b. It's my job to take the call.

   c. Every call is an opportunity, not an interruption.

8. When a caller is upset

   a. interrupt him before he gets more upset talking about it.

   b. wait until he has finished expressing his feelings and use the F-F-F technique.

   c. wait until he has finished speaking, then say anything to calm him down.

9. If you find yourself in a situation of having "phonephobia," you should
   a. change your Bs (beliefs).
   b. avoid using the phone.
   c. disguise your voice on the phone.

10. When you use the welcome approach, you should
   a. help your callers feel welcome.
   b. invite your callers to come to your facility.
   c. ask your callers if you can visit them.

Business Skills Express Series

This growing series of books addresses a broad range of key business skills and topics to meet the needs of employees, human resource departments, and training consultants.

To obtain information about these and other Business Skills Express books, please contact the Director of Special Sales, McGraw-Hill, 11 West 19th Street, New York, NY 10011.

Effective Performance Management
ISBN   1-55623-867-3

Hiring the Best
ISBN   1-55623-865-7

Writing that Works
ISBN   1-55623-856-8

Customer Service Excellence
ISBN   1-55623-969-6

Writing for Business Results
ISBN   1-55623-854-1

Powerful Presentation Skills
ISBN   1-55623-870-3

Meetings that Work
ISBN   1-55623-866-5

Effective Teamwork
ISBN   1-55623-880-0

Time Management
ISBN   1-55623-888-6

Assertiveness Skills
ISBN   1-55623-857-6

Motivation at Work
ISBN   1-55623-868-1

Overcoming Anxiety at Work
ISBN   1-55623-869-X

Positive Politics at Work
ISBN   1-55623-879-7

Telephone Skills at Work
ISBN   1-55623-858-4

Managing Conflict at Work
ISBN   1-55623-890-8

The New Supervisor: Skills for Success
ISBN   1-55623-762-6

The *Americans with Disabilities Act*: What Supervisors Need to Know
ISBN   1-55623-889-4

Managing the Demands of Work and Home
ISBN   0-7863-0221-6

Effective Listening Skills
ISBN   0-7863-0122-8

Goal Management at Work
ISBN   0-7863-0225-9

Positive Attitudes at Work
ISBN   0-7863-0167-8

Supervising the Difficult Employee
ISBN   0-7863-0219-4

Cultural Diversity in the Workplace
ISBN   0-7863-0125-2

Managing Organizational Change
ISBN   0-7863-0162-7

Negotiating for Business Results
ISBN   0-7863-0114-7

Practical Business Communication
ISBN   0-7863-0227-5

High Performance Speaking
ISBN   0-7863-0222-4

Delegation Skills
ISBN   0-7863-0148-1

Coaching Skills: A Guide for Supervisors
ISBN   0-7863-0220-8

Customer Service and the Telephone
ISBN   0-7863-0224-0

Creativity at Work
ISBN   0-7863-0223-2

Effective Interpersonal Relationships
ISBN   0-7863-0255-0

The Participative Leader
ISBN   0-7863-0252-6

Building Customer Loyalty
ISBN   0-7863-0253-4

Getting and Staying Organized
ISBN   0-7863-0254-2

Multicultural Customer Service
ISBN   0-7863-0332-8

Business Etiquette
ISBN   0-7863-0323-9

Empowering Employees
ISBN   0-7863-0314-X

Training Skills for Supervisors
ISBN   0-7863-0313-1

Moving Meetings
ISBN   0-7863-0333-6